All about
RAVENS

Ravens have black feathers.

Ravens are very smart and strong.

Ravens like to play in the wind.

Ravens make loud noises and talk to each other.

Ravens show hunters where to find polar bears.

Ravens are scavengers.

Ravens build their nests in high places.

There are a lot of
ravens in Nunavut!